MEL BAY'S
Easy Way to Guitar A

PREFACE

EASYWAY TO GUITAR IS A THREE-BOOK COURSE WHICH IS CAREFULLY DESIGNED TO GIVE THE GUITAR STUDENT AN EASY-TO-UNDERSTAND YET THOROUGH GROUNDING IN THE BASICS. THIS POPULAR COURSE IS BUILT ON CONCEPTS OF NOTE READING AND SOLO PERFORMANCE. CHORD PLAYING IS GRADUALLY INTRODUCED. AN IDEAL CHORD PLAYING SUPPLEMENT TO THIS METHOD IS *MEL BAY'S FUN WITH THE GUITAR*. UPON COMPLETION OF THE THREE BOOKS IN THIS SERIES, THE GUITAR STUDENT MAY CONTINUE STUDY IN *MEL BAY'S MODERN GUITAR METHOD BOOK 2.*

Video
dv.melbay.com/93194EB

You Tube
www.melbay.com/93194V

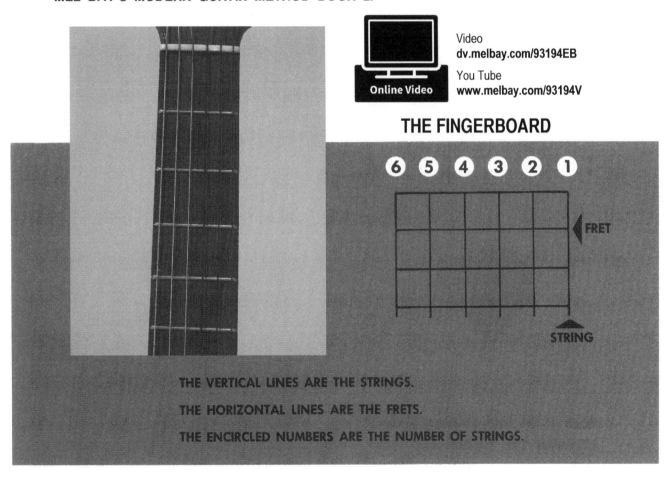

THE FINGERBOARD

THE VERTICAL LINES ARE THE STRINGS.

THE HORIZONTAL LINES ARE THE FRETS.

THE ENCIRCLED NUMBERS ARE THE NUMBER OF STRINGS.

THE CORRECT
WAY TO HOLD
THE GUITAR

THIS IS THE PICK

HOLD IT IN THIS MANNER FIRMLY
BETWEEN THE THUMB AND FIRST
FINGER.

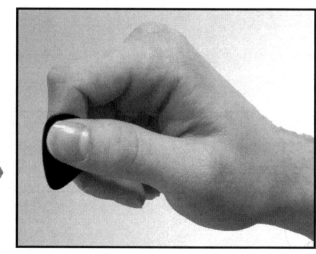

STRIKING THE STRINGS

⊓ = DOWN STROKE OF
THE PICK

THE LEFT HAND POSITION

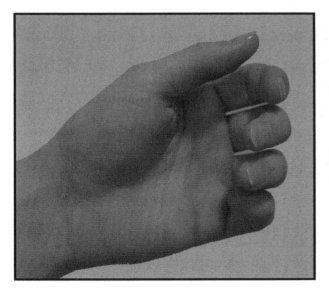

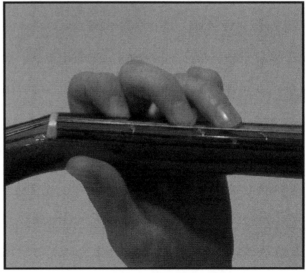

PLACE YOUR FINGERS FIRMLY ON THE STRINGS DIRECTLY BEHIND THE FRETS.

TUNING THE GUITAR

The six open strings of the guitar will be of the same pitch as the six notes shown in the illustration of the piano keyboard. Note that five of the strings are below the middle C of the piano keyboard.

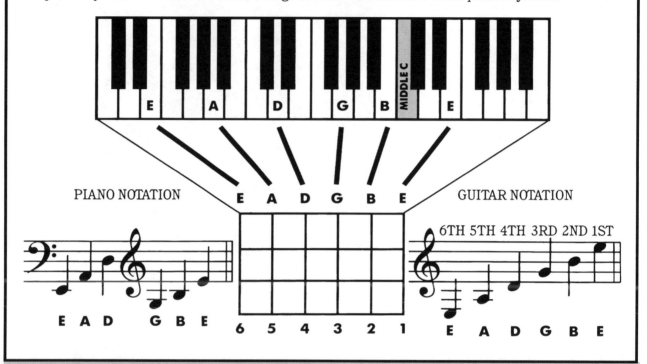

PIANO NOTATION

E A D G B E

GUITAR NOTATION

6TH 5TH 4TH 3RD 2ND 1ST

E A D G B E

6 5 4 3 2 1

ANOTHER METHOD OF TUNING

1. Tune the 6th string in unison with the **E** or 12th white key to the LEFT of MIDDLE C on the piano.

2. Place the finger behind the fifth fret of the 6th string. This will give you the tone or pitch of the 5th string **(A).**

3. Place finger behind the fifth fret of the 5th string to get the pitch of the 4th string **(D).**

4. Repeat same procedure to obtain the pitch of the 3rd string **(G).**

5. Place finger behind the fourth fret of the 3rd string to get the pitch of the 2nd string **(B).**

6. Place finger behind the fifth fret of the 2nd string to get the pitch of the 1st string **(E).**

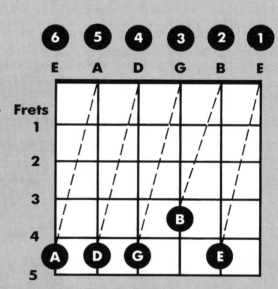

ELECTRONIC GUITAR TUNER

Electronic Guitar Tuners are available at your music store. They are a handy device and highly recommended.

THE RUDIMENTS OF MUSIC

THE STAFF: Music is written on a STAFF consisting of FIVE LINES and FOUR SPACES. The lines and spaces are numbered upward as shown:

```
5TH LINE ————————————————————
                               4TH SPACE
4TH LINE ————————————————————
                               3RD SPACE
3RD LINE ————————————————————
                               2ND SPACE
2ND LINE ————————————————————
                               1ST SPACE
1ST LINE ————————————————————
```

THE LINES AND SPACES ARE NAMED AFTER LETTERS OF THE ALPHABET.

The **LINES** are named as follows:

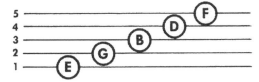

The letters can easily be remembered by the sentence — Every Good Boy Does Fine

The letter-names of the **SPACES** are:

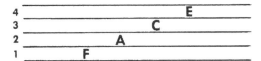

They spell the word **F-A-C-E**

The musical alphabet has seven letters — A B C D E F G

The **STAFF** is divided into measures by vertical lines called **BARS**

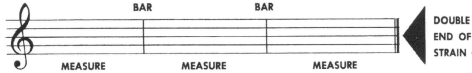

DOUBLE BARS MARK THE END OF A SECTION OR STRAIN OF MUSIC.

THE CLEF:

THIS SIGN IS THE TREBLE OR G CLEF.

ALL GUITAR MUSIC WILL BE WRITTEN IN THIS CLEF.

THE SECOND LINE OF THE TREBLE CLEF IS KNOWN AS THE G LINE. MANY PEOPLE CALL THE TREBLE CLEF THE G CLEF BECAUSE IT CIRCLES AROUND THE G LINE.

THE TYPES OF NOTES

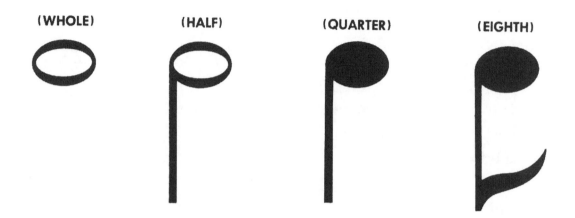

(WHOLE)   (HALF)   (QUARTER)   (EIGHTH)

THE TYPE OF NOTE WILL INDICATE THE LENGTH OF ITS SOUND.

THIS IS A WHOLE NOTE. THE HEAD IS HOLLOW.
IT DOES NOT HAVE A STEM.

= 4 BEATS
A WHOLE-NOTE WILL RECEIVE FOUR BEATS OR COUNTS.

THIS IS A HALF NOTE THE HEAD IS HOLLOW.
IT HAS A STEM.

= 2 BEATS
A HALF-NOTE WILL RECEIVE TWO BEATS OR COUNTS.

THIS IS A QUARTER NOTE THE HEAD IS SOLID.
IT HAS A STEM.

= 1 BEAT
A QUARTER NOTE WILL RECEIVE ONE BEAT OR COUNT.

THIS IS AN EIGHTH NOTE THE HEAD IS SOLID.
IT HAS A STEM AND A FLAG.

= ½ BEAT
AN EIGHTH-NOTE WILL RECEIVE ONE-HALF BEAT OR COUNT. (2 FOR 1 BEAT)

RESTS

A REST IS A SIGN USED TO DESIGNATE A PERIOD OF SILENCE. THIS PERIOD OF SILENCE WILL BE OF THE SAME DURATION OF TIME AS THE NOTE TO WHICH IT CORRESPONDS.

 THIS IS AN EIGHTH REST

 THIS IS A QUARTER REST

THIS IS A HALF REST   NOTE THAT IT LAYS ON THE LINE.

THIS IS A WHOLE REST   NOTE THAT IT HANGS DOWN FROM THE LINE.

NOTES

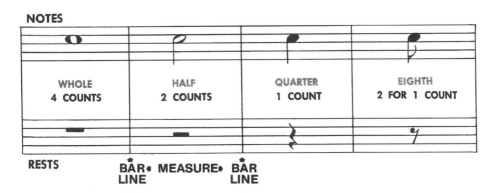

| WHOLE 4 COUNTS | HALF 2 COUNTS | QUARTER 1 COUNT | EIGHTH 2 FOR 1 COUNT |

RESTS   BAR• MEASURE• BAR
           LINE   LINE

BAR-LINES DIVIDE THE STAFF INTO MEASURES.

THE TIME SIGNATURE

THE ABOVE EXAMPLES ARE THE COMMON TYPES OF TIME SIGNATURES TO BE USED IN THIS BOOK.

$\frac{4}{4}$ THE TOP NUMBER INDICATES THE NUMBER OF BEATS PER MEASURE.

$\frac{4}{4}$ THE BOTTOM NUMBER INDICATES THE TYPE OF NOTE RECEIVING ONE BEAT.

$\frac{4}{4}$ BEATS PER MEASURE

$\frac{4}{4}$ A QUARTER-NOTE RECEIVES ONE BEAT

A LARGE C THIS:  SIGNIFIES SO CALLED "COMMON TIME" AND IS SIMPLY ANOTHER WAY OF DESIGNATING $\frac{4}{4}$ TIME.

THE NOTES ON THE FIRST STRING (E)

THREE NOTES ON THE 1ST STRING:

PRESS THE FINGER FIRMLY BEHIND THE FRETS.

NEVER PLACE THE FINGER ON THE FRETS.

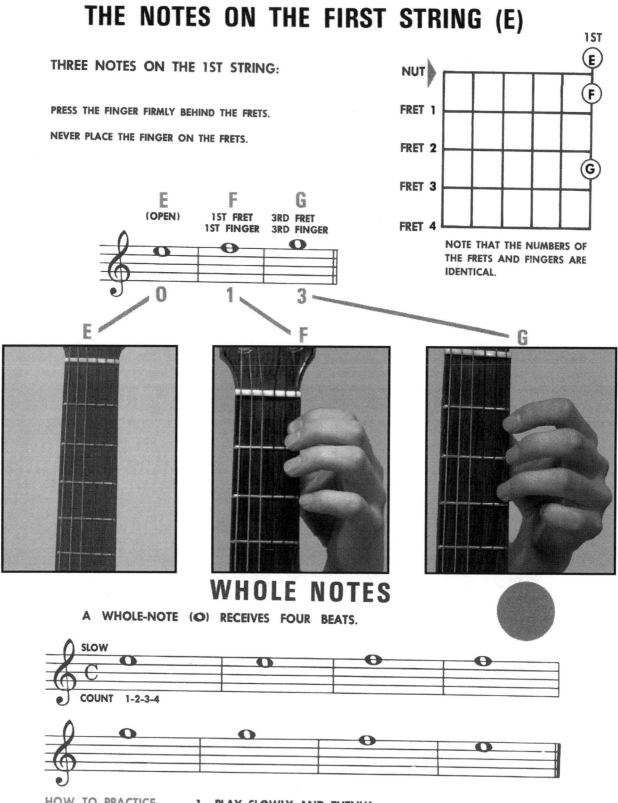

E (OPEN)   F 1ST FRET 1ST FINGER   G 3RD FRET 3RD FINGER

0   1   3

E   F   G

1ST

NUT ▶

FRET 1

FRET 2

FRET 3

FRET 4

NOTE THAT THE NUMBERS OF THE FRETS AND FINGERS ARE IDENTICAL.

WHOLE NOTES

A WHOLE-NOTE (O) RECEIVES FOUR BEATS.

SLOW

COUNT 1-2-3-4

HOW TO PRACTICE

1. PLAY SLOWLY AND EVENLY.

2. PLACE YOUR FINGERS FIRMLY ON THE STRINGS DIRECTLY BEHIND THE FRETS.

3. BE RELAXED AT ALL TIMES.

8

HALF NOTES

A HALF-NOTE (♩) RECEIVES TWO BEATS

COUNT: 1 -2 - 3 -4

1 2 (3 4)

QUARTER NOTES

REST

A QUARTER-NOTE (♩) RECEIVES ONE BEAT

COUNT 1   2   3   4

1   2   3   (4)

THE MIXMASTER

COUNT 1 2 3 4

(REST)   (REST)   (REST)

NOTES ON THE FIRST STRING

(FILL IN THE BLOCKS)

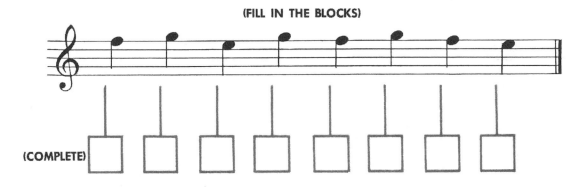

(COMPLETE)

9

OUR FIRST CHORDS

Easyway "C"

E - Z "C"   PLAY OPEN

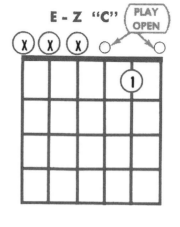

Easyway "G7"

E - Z "G7"

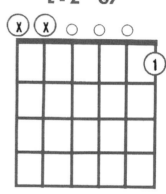

(X) = Indicates that the string is
to be omitted.

Practice the above Chords
until the tone is clear.

/ / / /   Strokes of the Pick, Thumb,
or Index Finger down across
the strings.

INDEX FINGER STRUM

THUMB STRUM

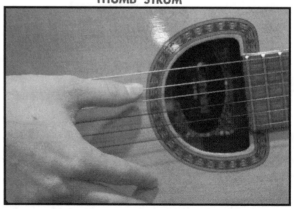

SING-A-LONG SONG
YELLOW ROSE OF TEXAS

STUDENT:
Strum
Chords

TEACHER:
Play
Melody

C

She's the sweetest col- or a Fel- low ev- er knew. Her

G7

eyes are bright as dia- monds, they Spark- le like the dew. You may

C

talk a- bout your dear- est maid's and sing of Ro- sa- Lee, but my

G7   C   G7   C

Yel- low Rose of Tex - as is the best you'll ev- er see.

THE NOTES ON THE SECOND STRING (B)

THREE NOTES ON THE 2ND STRING:

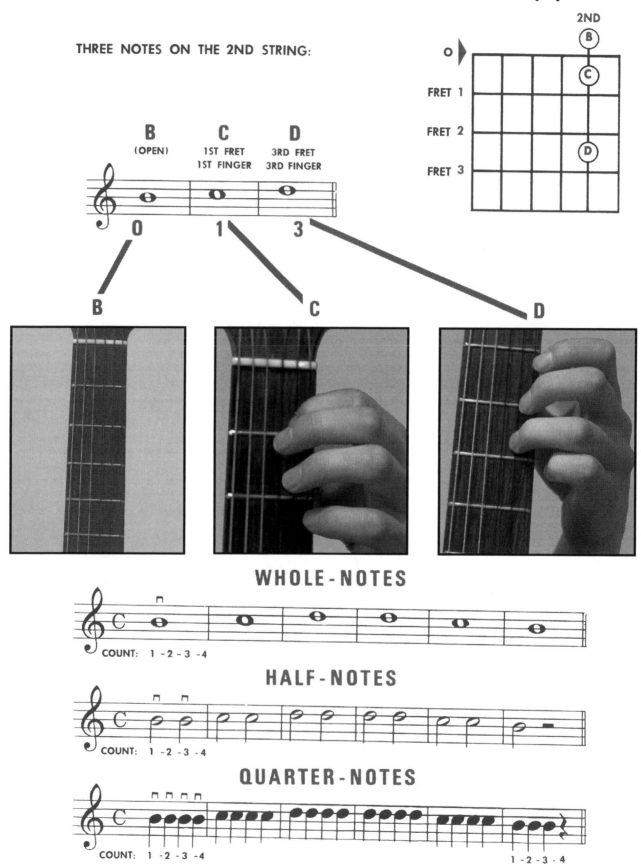

WHOLE-NOTES

COUNT: 1 - 2 - 3 - 4

HALF-NOTES

COUNT: 1 - 2 - 3 - 4

QUARTER-NOTES

COUNT: 1 - 2 - 3 - 4   1 - 2 - 3 - 4

12

THREE-FOUR TIME

THIS SIGN  INDICATES THREE-FOUR TIME.

$\frac{3}{4}$ — BEATS PER MEASURE. [MEASURE = DISTANCE BETWEEN THE BARS]

— TYPE OF NOTE RECEIVING ONE BEAT (QUARTER NOTE).

REMEMBER IN THREE-FOUR TIME, WE WILL HAVE THREE BEATS PER MEASURE.

A QUARTER NOTE WILL RECEIVE ONE BEAT.

THE RULE OF THE DOT

A DOT PLACED AFTER A NOTE OR A REST INCREASES ITS TIME VALUE BY ONE HALF.

EXAMPLES

♩ = 2 COUNTS   ♩• = 3 COUNTS   ♩ = 1 COUNT   ♩• = 1½ COUNTS

THE MERRY MEN

A DOTTED HALF-NOTE ♩• WILL RECEIVE THREE BEATS.

SING A-LONG IN 3/4 TIME
STRUM SONG

Sing- ing and Play- ing is Fun, You see.

Count- ing and Strum- ming come Nat- urall- y.

Sing- ing and Play- ing will al- ways be,

eas- y and Fun when they're done by me.

ANOTHER SING-A-LONG SONG
MARY ANN

All day, all night, Ma-ry Ann,

Down by the sea-side, Sift-in' Sand.

All the lit-tle Child-dren Love Ma-ry Ann,

Down by the sea-side, Sift-in' Sand.

THE NOTES ON THE THIRD STRING (G)

TWO NOTES ON THE 3RD STRING:

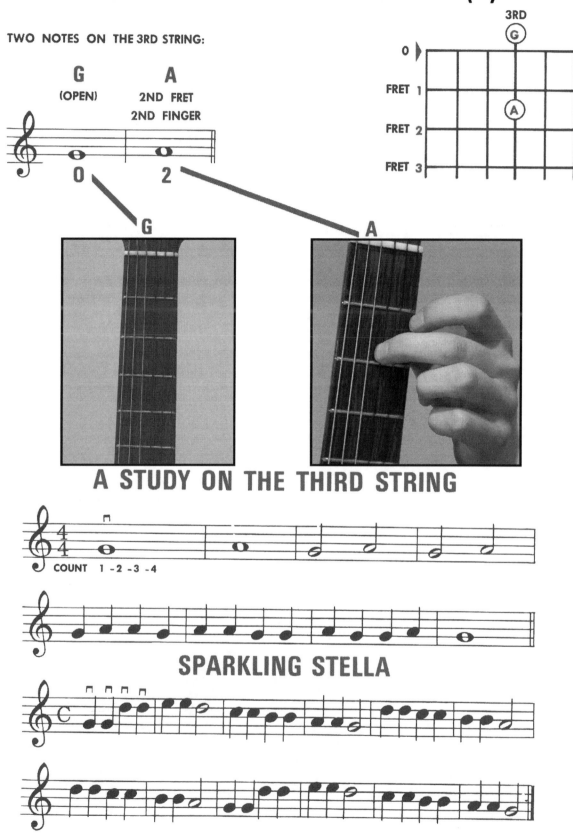

A STUDY ON THE THIRD STRING

COUNT 1 - 2 - 3 - 4

SPARKLING STELLA

SOLOS ON THE FIRST, SECOND AND THIRD STRINGS
MARCH OF THE MOON PATROL

GEE-BEE

COUNT: 1 2 3 4

A SURPRISE FOR MR. HAYDN

17

INTRODUCING THE . . . .

Note

5TH FRET
4TH FINGER

A

5

THE FIRST STRING WALTZ

THE LITTLE FINGER WALTZ

ANOTHER CHORD

Easyway "F"

E - Z "F"

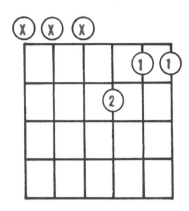

JACOB'S LADDER

We are Climb-ing Ja-cob's Lad-der, We are

Climb-ing Ja-cob's Lad-der, We are Climb-ing

Ja-cob's Lad-der, Sol-diers of the Lord.

2. *Rise, Shine, Give God Glory*

THIS TRAIN

C   G7   C

This Train is bound for Glo-ry This Train.

SPIRITUAL

This Train is bound for Glo-ry This Train.

C   F   C

This Train is bound for Glo-ry on-ly takes the Good and Ho-ly

G7   C F   C

This Train is bound for Glo-ry This Train.

20

THE NOTES ON THE FOURTH STRING (D)

THREE NOTES ON THE 4TH STRING:

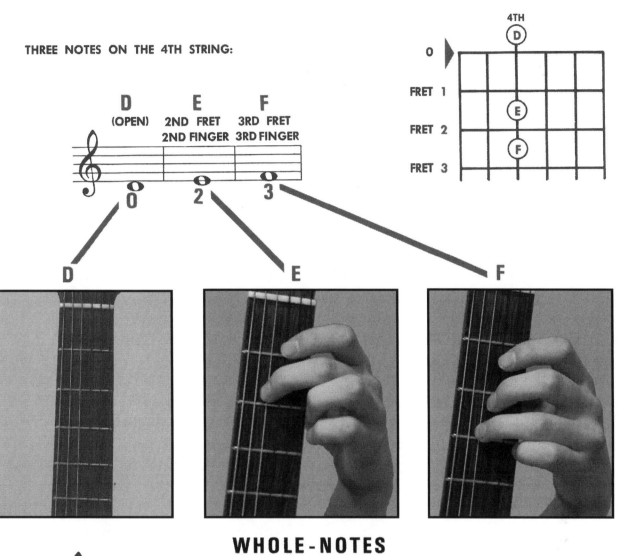

WHOLE-NOTES

COUNT: 1 - 2 - 3 - 4

HALF-NOTES

(REST)

COUNT: 1 - 2 - 3 - 4   1   2   (3   4)

QUARTER-NOTES

COUNT: 1 — 2 — 3 — 4

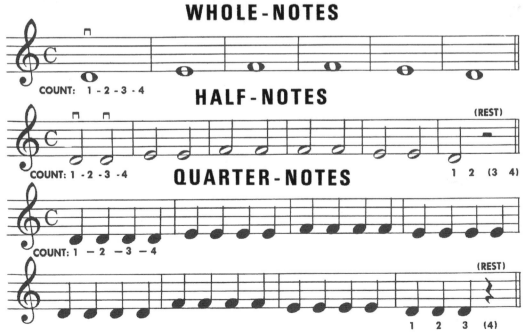

(REST)

1   2   3   (4)

HAPPY SONG

OLD McDONALD'S FARM

NOTES ON THE 4TH STRING

THE NOTES ON THE FIFTH STRING (A)

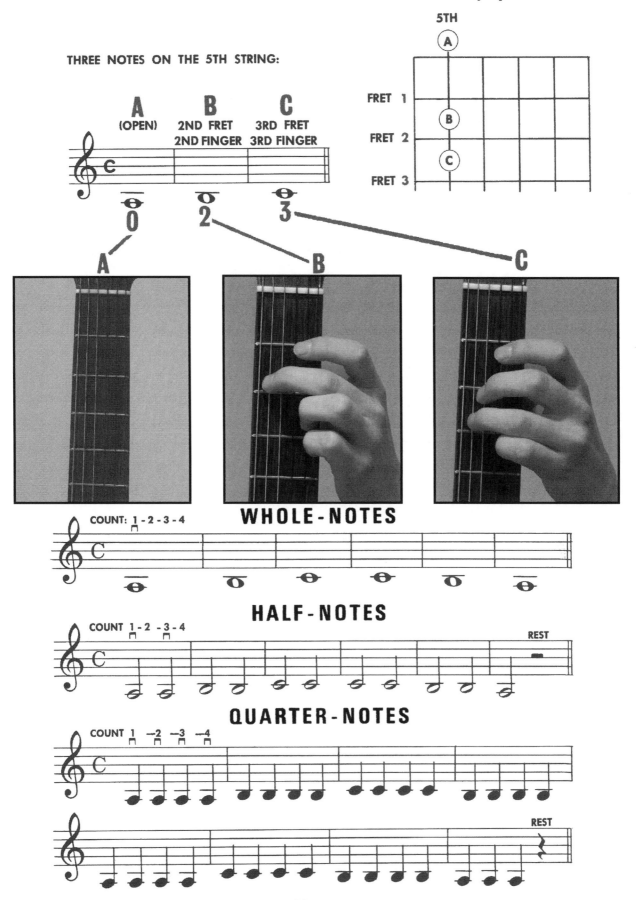

THREE NOTES ON THE 5TH STRING:

A (OPEN) **B** 2ND FRET 2ND FINGER **C** 3RD FRET 3RD FINGER

5TH

A

FRET 1

B

FRET 2

C

FRET 3

A   B   C

WHOLE-NOTES

COUNT: 1 - 2 - 3 - 4

HALF-NOTES

COUNT 1 - 2 - 3 - 4

REST

QUARTER-NOTES

COUNT 1 - 2 - 3 - 4

REST

23

THE TEXAS WALTZ

LONDON BRIDGE

NOTES ON THE 5TH STRING

(COMPLETE)

24

THE NOTES ON THE SIXTH STRING (E)

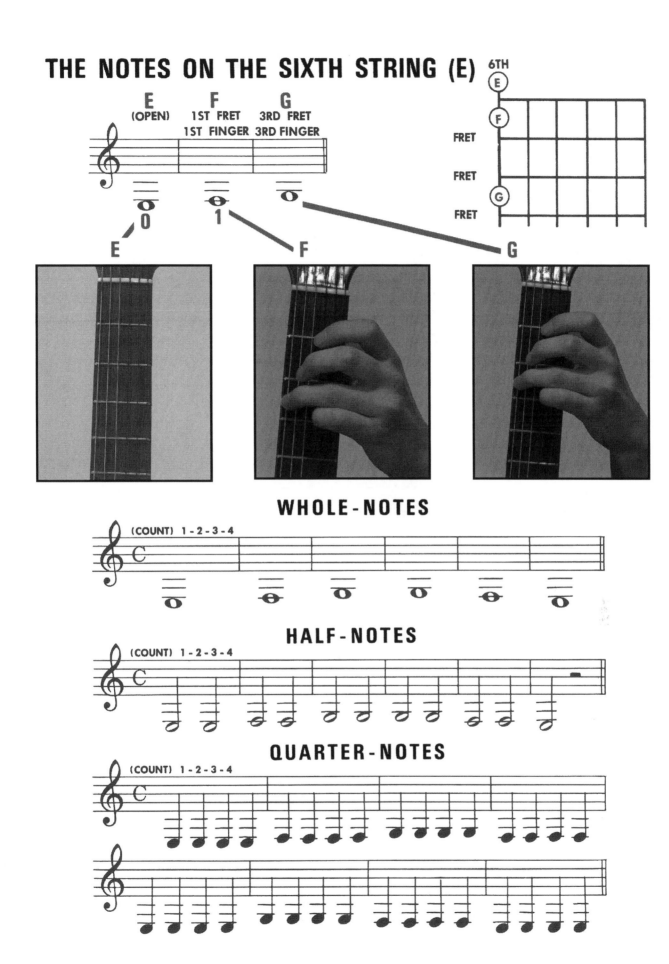

WHOLE-NOTES

HALF-NOTES

QUARTER-NOTES

NOTES ON THE 6th STRING

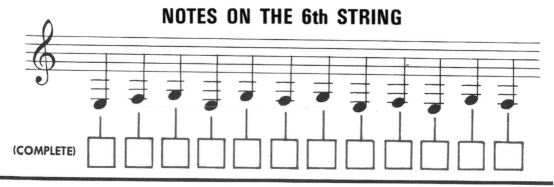

(COMPLETE)

THE NOTES ON THE E-(6), A-(5), & D-(4) STRINGS

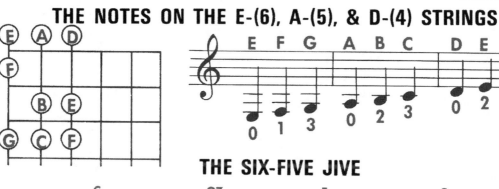

THE SIX-FIVE JIVE

HITTING ON ALL SIX

COUNT: 1 2 3 4

A REVIEW OF THE EIGHTEEN BASIC NOTES

(INSERT THE ALPHABET LETTERS AND FRET NUMBERS)

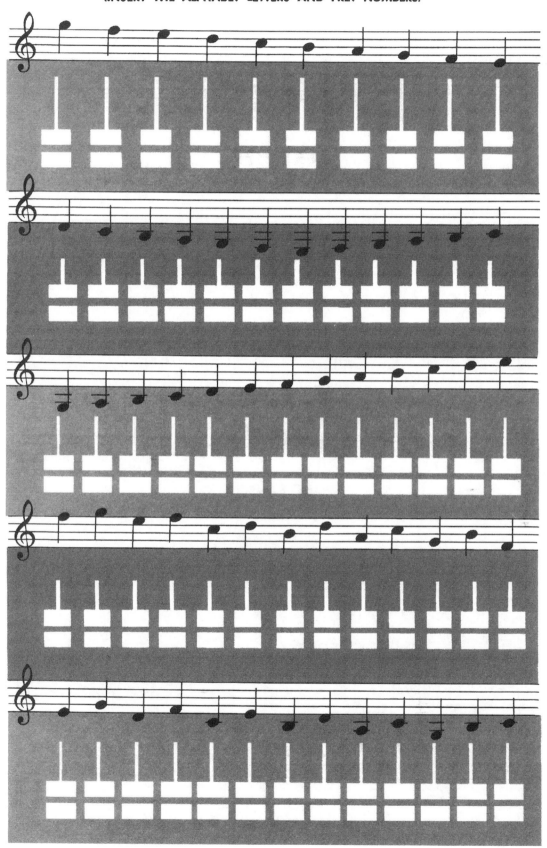

REVIEW OF THE NOTES ON THE GUITAR IN THE
FIRST POSITION

TAKE OFF

JET FLIGHT

28

THE REPEAT
DOTS BEFORE AND AFTER A DOUBLE BAR MEAN REPEAT THE MEASURES BETWEEN.

THE REPEATER

THE PICNIC

REPEAT FROM THE BEGINNING

29

THE TIE

THE TIE IS A CURVED LINE BETWEEN TWO NOTES OF THE SAME PITCH.
THE FIRST NOTE IS PLAYED AND HELD FOR THE TIME DURATION OF
BOTH. THE SECOND NOTE IS NOT PLAYED BUT HELD.

EXAMPLE

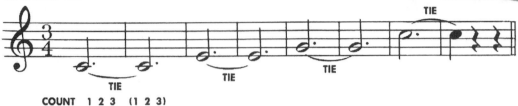

COUNT 1 2 3 (1 2 3)

FATHER TIME

WHERE OH WHERE HAS MY LITTLE DOG GONE?

30

PICK-UP NOTES

THE NOTES AT THE BEGINNING OF A STRAIN BEFORE THE FIRST MEASURE ARE REFERRED TO AS PICK-UP NOTES. THE RHYTHM FOR PICK-UP NOTES IS TAKEN FROM THE LAST MEASURE OF THE SELECTION AND THE BEATS ARE COUNTED AS SUCH. (NOTE THE TWO BEATS IN THE LAST MEASURE.)

RED RIVER VALLEY

COMIN' 'ROUND THE MOUNTAIN

31

WHEN TWO OR MORE NOTES ARE WRITTEN
ON THE SAME STEM PLAY THEM AS ONE.

EXAMPLE:

(X - - - - - - -): HOLD FINGERS DOWN. NEVER RAISE FINGERS UNTIL NECESSARY.

SEEING DOUBLE

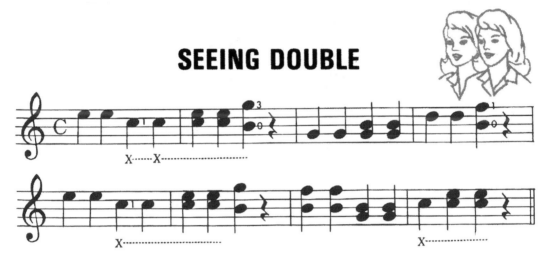

TIC TOC

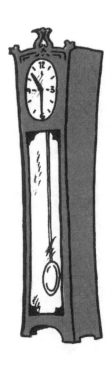

32

ANOTHER SING-A-LONG SONG
AMAZING GRACE

(Play the Solo Part One Time and the Chord Accompaniment Another)

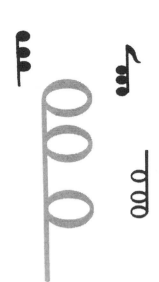

CHORDS

A MELODY IS A SUCCESSION OF SINGLE TONES.

A CHORD IS A COMBINATION OF TONES SOUNDED TOGETHER

TONES IN A MELODY   THE SAME TONES AS A CHORD.

WE WILL CONSTRUCT OUR CHORDS BY PLAYING THE CHORDAL TONES SEPARATELY AS IN A MELODY AND WITHOUT RAISING THE FINGERS, STRIKING THEM TOGETHER.

FIRST CHORD WALTZ

FIRST DUET

STUDENT SHOULD PLAY BOTH PARTS

SOLO

ACCOMPANI-MENT

AN INSIDE CHORD WALTZ
REST THE PICK AGAINST THE FIRST STRING

THE BUILDER

CHILDREN'S SONG

35

BASS SOLOS WITH CHORD ACCOMPANIMENT

WHEN PLAYING BASS SOLOS WITH CHORD ACCOMPANIMENT YOU WILL FIND THE SOLO WITH THE STEMS TURNED DOWNWARD AND THE ACCOMPANIMENT WITH THE STEMS TURNED UPWARD.

COUNT: 1   2   3

IN THE EXAMPLE SHOWN ABOVE YOU SEE THE DOTTED HALF-NOTE (E) WITH THE STEM DOWNWARD. IT IS PLAYED ON THE COUNT OF ONE AND IS HELD FOR COUNTS TWO AND THREE.

THE QUARTER REST OVER THE DOTTED HALF-NOTE INDICATES THAT THERE IS NO CHORD ACCOMPANIMENT AT THE COUNT OF ONE. THE CHORDS WITH THE STEMS UPWARD ARE PLAYED ON COUNTS OF TWO AND THREE.

THE GUITAR WALTZ

36

MY VALENTINE

GUITAR FOR TWO

FIRST AND SECOND ENDINGS

SOMETIMES TWO ENDINGS ARE REQUIRED IN CERTAIN SELECTIONS . . ONE TO LEAD BACK INTO A REPEATED CHORUS AND ONE TO CLOSE IT.

THEY WILL BE SHOWN LIKE THIS.

THE FIRST TIME PLAY THE BRACKETED ENDING 1. REPEAT THE CHORUS. THE SECOND TIME SKIP THE FIRST ENDING AND PLAY ENDING NO. 2.

CHOPSTICKS

38

♯ SHARPS, ♭ FLATS, AND ♮ NATURALS

THE DISTANCE FROM ONE FRET TO THE NEXT IS A HALF STEP. TWO HALF STEPS MAKE A WHOLE STEP.

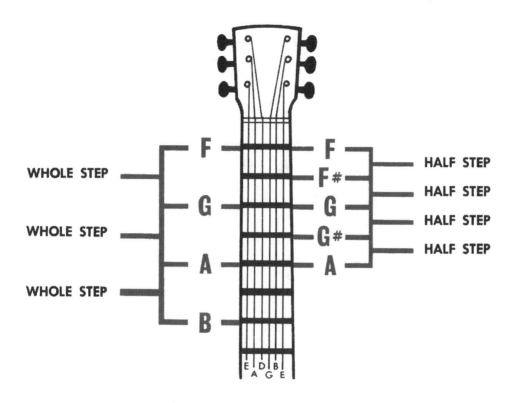

HALF STEPS ONE FRET BETWEEN ● WHOLE STEPS TWO FRETS APART

 SHARPS ♯ RAISE THE NOTE A HALF STEP. PLAY THE NEXT FRET HIGHER.

 FLATS ♭ LOWER THE NOTE A HALF STEP. IF THE NOTE IS AN OPEN STRING, PLAY THE FLAT ON THE FOURTH FRET OF THE NEXT LOWER STRING. ONE EXCEPTION IS THE B NOTE ON THE OPEN SECOND STRING. THE B FLAT IS PLAYED ON THE THIRD STRING, THIRD FRET.

 NATURALS ♮ CANCEL A PREVIOUS ♯ OR ♭

THE SHARP

A SHARP PLACED BEFORE A NOTE RAISES IT ONE FRET.

SHARPIE

"COUNTRY BOY"

THE FLAT

A FLAT PLACED BEFORE A NOTE LOWERS IT ONE FRET.

MR. FLAT TOP

L'IL LIZA JANE

41

THE NATURAL

A NATURAL PLACED BEFORE A NOTE RESTORES THAT NOTE TO ITS NATURAL OR REGULAR POSITION.

A PAIR OF NATURALS

SWEET BETSY FROM PIKE

A REVIEW OF SHARPS, FLATS AND NATURALS

♯ —THIS IS A SHARP, IT RAISES A NOTE ONE FRET.

♭ —THIS IS A FLAT, IT LOWERS A NOTE ONE FRET.

♮ —THIS IS A NATURAL, IT RESTORES A NOTE TO ORIGINAL PITCH.

REMEMBER: THE FRET NUMBER AND THE LEFT HAND FINGERS ARE IDENTICAL.

"THE MIXUP"

BILLY BOY

43

THE CHROMATIC SCALE

THE CHROMATIC SCALE IS FORMED EXCLUSIVELY OF HALF STEPS. ASCENDING, THE CHROMATIC SCALE USES SHARPS, (♯), THE DESCENDING SCALE USES FLATS, (♭).

CONCERTO

GUITAR DUET **FOLLOW THE LEADER**

STUDENT SHOULD PLAY BOTH PARTS

COUNT: 2 3 4 | 1 2 3 4

THE EIGHTH NOTE

AN EIGHTH NOTE RECEIVES ONE-HALF BEAT. (ONE QUARTER NOTE EQUALS TWO EIGHTH NOTES.)

AN EIGHTH NOTE WILL HAVE A HEAD, STEM, AND FLAG. IF TWO OR MORE ARE IN SUCCESSIVE ORDER THEY MAY BE CONNECTED BY A BAR. (SEE EXAMPLE)

EIGHTH NOTES AND EIGHTH RESTS

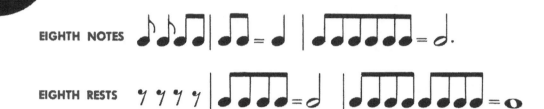

EIGHTH NOTES

EIGHTH RESTS

THE SCALE IN EIGHTH NOTES

COUNT 1 & 2 & 3 & 4 & 1 & 2 & 3 & 4 &

I'VE BEEN WORKIN' ON THE RAILROAD

COUNT 1   2   3 & 4 &

46

THIS OLD MAN

HOP-A-LONG

LONGING FOR THE MOUNTAINS

NORWEGIAN FOLK SONG

PROCEED TO BOOK "B" OF THIS COURSE

Made in the USA
San Bernardino, CA
16 October 2016